JOHN GOBLIKON'S
GUIDE TO LIVING YOUR BEST LIFE

JOHN GOBLIKON'S
GUIDE TO LIVING YOUR BEST LIFE

by John Goblikon

with Brandon Dermer and Dave Rispoli —— Foreword by Wes Borland of Limp Bizkit

A GENUINE RARE BIRD BOOK

LOS ANGELES, CALIF.

THIS IS A GENUINE RARE BIRD BOOK

A Rare Bird Book | Rare Bird Books
453 South Spring Street, Suite 302
Los Angeles, CA 90013
rarebirdbooks.com

FIRST PAPERBACK EDITION

For more information, address:
Rare Bird Books Subsidiary Rights Department
453 South Spring Street, Suite 302
Los Angeles, CA 90013

Set in Minion
Printed in the United States

10 9 8 7 6 5 4 3 2 1

Publisher's Cataloging-in-Publication Data

Names: Goblikon, John, author. | Dermer, Brandon, author.
| Rispoli, Dave, author.
Title: John Goblikon's Guide to Living Your Best Life / by John Goblikon;
with Brandon Dermer and Dave Rispoli.
Description: First Paperback Edition. | New York, NY; Los Angeles, CA:
Rare Bird Books, 2019.
Identifiers: ISBN 9781644282304
Subjects: LCSH Nekrogoblikon. | Self-help techniques—Humor.
| Self-realization—Humor. | Success—Humor. | Parodies. | Humorous stories. |
BISAC HUMOR / Form / Parodies
Classification: LCC PN6231.S83 .G63 2019 | DDC 818/.5402—dc23

*This book is definitely **not** dedicated to my assistant, Jerry.*

FOREWORD

By Wes Borland

To whom it may concern (and if you are concerned with this publication in any way, may God have mercy on your soul):

It's been sixty-one days since John Goblikon locked me away in his dungeon, a dark and musty stone room, dripping with moisture, completely bare save for one disheveled poster depicting the eighties glam metal band Winger. In this poster, Kip Winger's luscious hairy chest is revealed by a low-cut, white, tiger-print spandex top. My only entertainment has been a worn VHS copy of *Weekend at Bernie's* that I've watched countless times now through a grime-covered top-loading VCR and television set. At first I wasn't sure why I was being held against my will, but it was eventually revealed to me—albeit through a series of skits, that John would come down and perform every three days, completely by himself, with no props or musical accompaniment—that my only hope for freedom was to write a foreword for this completely insane and self-indulgent "book." I could praise him for his rapier wit if rapiers were pool noodles, but they most certainly are not. I have learned of his ways and can only appreciate his love for tiki bars and metal music.

About halfway into my captivity, John brought down a blue Ikea bag full of an assortment of three-ring binders, sealed stacks of notebook paper, pens, boxes of donuts, gummy worms, a signed photo of Rick Springfield, and a Dungeons & Dragons Monster Manual. In his other hand, he carried a delicious pitcher of freshly made Long Island Iced Tea. After placing the items before me on the dungeon floor, he pulled a single white sugar packet from his pocket and handed it to me, simply saying: "You dropped your name tag…now get to work bitch." Having not had any food for days, I immediately went for the donuts. They were mostly powdered and filled with raspberry jam. I followed that by downing the entire pitcher of LIIT after dumping in the gummy worms. The drunken sugar high coma that came over me took me to a quiet palm tree–dotted beach. Everything was still beside a soft jasmine-scented breeze that rustled and purred through the palm fronds. Silky clouds lazily rested against the deep blue. I pushed my toes into the sand, looked over at Danny Glover, and said: "They say you are what you eat, but I don't remember John Goblikon eating a fucking legend."

INTRODUCTION

Goblin?

WOW! I'VE WRITTEN A BOOK! Well, I'm assuming that because, if you're reading these words—either out loud or to yourself—it means I have, in fact, actually *written* my book, finally. Who would've thought? Ya know, one day you're an internet-famous mid-level insurance salesman touring the planet with the world's premiere goblin metal band, Nekrogoblikon, and the next thing you know you're an *author*. Move over Shakespeare, John is an *author* now! What's that, Edgar Allen Poe? Can't hear you over the sound of all the new *book* money I'm counting right now…well, that, and because you're in a coffin. Oh, hey, Michelle Obama…yeah, we'll have to reschedule lunch next week…I'm on a big book tour right now…oh, *you've* written a book, too…that's cool.

At this point, I'm sure you're asking yourself, *how did I become an author living his best life?* One word: *Goblin.* Well, *living my life like a goblin*…so *six* words, actually. But you get it. Let me explain…

In a world filled with trolls, it's time to go green and live your life more like a goblin. *You deserve it!* That's right! *You!* Person holding this book...or listening to this as an audiobook, reading along to the sound of my voice, my *soothing* voice...or consuming through whatever the future of reading is...probably putting a chip in your arm or something. But **RIGHT NOW**, you deserve to go green! What does that mean? To go *green*? To live your life like a *goblin*? Well, it means a lot of different things, which I will now list for you in bullet points:

- Be kind. Be green. Treat everyone with the same love and respect you would want to be treated with in return. Except for trolls. *F*ck trolls!* Am I right? Of course, I am! You're reading *my* dang book!
- Give no fricks, but also give all the fricks in the world at the same time.
- Live constantly with intense, all-consuming anxiety while also being forever eternally optimistic.
- Listen to metal. Specifically, *goblin* metal. Even more specifically, *Nekrogoblikon*. Don't get it twisted. Slipknot ain't paying for this book! There aren't any gimmicks *here*.

So make sure to read this book with an open mind and open heart (and an open wallet if you haven't purchased the vinyl audiobook and had a chance to experience those bonus chapters).

Basically, what I'm trying to say is: try to be the exact opposite of your racist uncle on Facebook...because *you* deserve to live your best life!

CHAPTER ONE

Life

GANDHI CLAIMS THAT EVERYTHING we do in life is meaningless, but it's very important that we do it. I don't know what the heck that means. I just try to live my life by two simple words: *live mas*, which many of you may know as Latin for "live more"—something I feel *obligated* to include now because my publisher, Rare Bird, thinks it's helpful to throw in these little tidbits. (Seriously, guys, I appreciate the editorial assistance, but I'm pretty sure I got this one here. I mean, there's a reason why *I'm* the author and *you're* the publisher. Know your role. Stay in your own lane. I'll appease it to an extent because I'm still waiting for my first advance payment— supposedly due on "acceptance," whatever that means. Uh, I'm pretty sure you're going to *accept* it because fans have already pre-ordered the book and vinyl, but *okay*.)

Now, where was I? Ah, yes. Buddha, on the other hand, claims to live is to suffer. *Disagree!* To eat uncooked chicken fajitas before a first date is to suffer. To be alive is *awesome!* Just think of all the benefits that come with being alive…you get to sleep, eat fully cooked food (for the most part), listen to metal, have friends (I have so many, refer to my Instagram @JohnGoblikon), watch movies and Netflix, drive, go to Chili's, listen to NEKROGOB-LIKON, travel, drink beers, listen to metal, love!

Throughout the rest of this book, I'm going to teach you how to live *your* best life. But remember, everyone's best life is relative… because what is best for you might be different for someone else… like, to me, *my* best life is going to a Nekrogoblikon concert, drinking five beers, then gorging myself at Chili's. For Brad, my boss at my day job, it's dropping, like, $3,000 at the exclusive members-only clubhouse while attempting to make out with an ex-Vine-star-turned-actress-turned-Tik-Tok-star. For all the band members of Nekrogoblikon, it's touring with Limp Bizkit, *which they've done*. You've seen Limp Bizkit's guitar player, right, Wes Borland? The guy that wrote the foreword to this book? Guy sure wears a lot of make-up...he should really consider changing his name to Wes *Girl*and. I bet that guy's best life is getting an unlimited supply of Sephora gift cards or something. *Ha!*

So, yeah, "living your best life" truly is in the eye of the beholder.

It's also important to look at each day as a gift. No matter how tough times may get, always find peace in the fact that you're alive. Think of how many people are *not* alive. Remember the 1990 film *Ghost* directed by Jerry Zucker and written by Bruce Joel Rubin? Of course, you do! That movie kicks ass! Well, *news flash*, the lead character in the movie...he's *dead*! Yep, sorry to burst your bubble. Also, in real life, he is no longer alive! Which is weird, Patrick Swayze played a ghost in a movie called *Ghost*...and now he's a...a ghost. That's *some* foreshadowing, Bruce.

Quick side note, since becoming an author I've purchased a few audiobooks—from my favorite audiobook company, Recorded Books and Tantor Media—on how to actually *write* a book since I have no time to actually *read* books. (*Who the hell still reads books anyway?*) I found there's actually a "tool" in writing called "foreshadowing." "Foreshadowing" means to *hint* at something that will happen *later*. Like a really rancid fart *foreshadowing* that you have to poop.

Okay, back to life. As I was saying, live life like each day is your last. Make every moment count. No matter how big or small the moment. Ordering Chili's To Go? *Make it count! Order the crap out of that menu!* Ya know what? Get that *extra* order of Southwestern Egg Rolls! *I'm* buying. (Note to legal and accounting: I am *not* buying.) Have a big test today? Study as long and as hard as you you're willing to do. Whether you get an A or an F, you made it count. [Note from Rare Bird: an F grade will only result in *failing* a test, as "F" is short for "Fail."]

Takeaway: Every moment, while alive, is a gift.

Another thing I'd like to touch on with this is that, as Eminem conveys quite authoritatively in his hit documentary *8 Mile*, "You only get one shot." He, of course, was referring to battle rapping and making it in the cutthroat rap game, but that same idea applies to the overall concept of "living your best life." You really do only get *one* life, even if you actually live multiple lives. It's all part of one greater vision of what life is…or what *Life* is. At least that's what *they* say. Regardless of what some metaphysical people might claim, nobody *really* knows what happens when we die. (Note: refer to chapter DEATH, which will be written later on—when I get around to it, but definitely *before* the book is *accepted*, so I can finally paid for this damn thing).

So I guess what I'm trying to say is that we all have to live each and every day to the fullest. Well, technically you don't *have* to do anything other than, like, eat, sleep, and listen to Nekrogoblikon. No, really. If you *don't* do *those* things, you *will* die, and that would be a ridiculous waste of life. Nope, come to think of it, I guess you also have to pay your bills, go to work, maintain relationships, pursue your passions, workout and take care of your body… Luckily for you, dear reader, I've written chapters touching on all of those explorative topics, so…Johnny's got ya covered.

Now, where was I? Ah, Life…capital L. With *Life* comes an abundance of trials and tribulations that will cause you stress and heartache, so…relax. *You've earned it!* You know that phrase, "I'll sleep when I'm dead"? No, thank you! I'll sleep…**RIGHT NOW**. I'll be *dead* when I'm dead. [Note from Rare Bird: Reader be advised, John tends to ramble, and/or get off track. We asked him to read up on the concept of "less is more," but he got confused and ended up screaming at his assistant, Jerry.] Sure, guys. *Still* waiting on that check… where less is *definitely* not more.

Anyway, next, I find that, when exploring a topic, it's important to seek as many "outside opinions" as possible before determining your own. That's why I've gathered a few of my favorite quotes from my peers, aka other celebrity-influencer-famous-types, to see what they had to say about this thing we call Life. I found some of the quotes to be philosophical, while others were more straightforward and inspiring. Most are confusing. All are just plain wrong. Lucky for you, I'm here to look at your world and make sense of it through my goblin eyes!

Life is like riding a bicycle. To keep your balance, you must keep moving.

—ALBERT EINSTEIN

Not really sure I one hundred percent agree with you there, Al. *Life* is more like riding a Segway: it doesn't make a lot of sense, seems completely pointless and unnecessary, but when you just get on and ride…it's fun as hell! Even though you look like an idiot doing it.

Nothing can dim the light that shines from within.

—MAYA ANGELOU

We are talking about *life* here Maya, not *lights*. Pfft. Maybe you need to *turn up* the lights so you can see what you're writing in my dang book!

You get in life what you have the courage to ask for.

—OPRAH WINFREY

I completely agree, O. This one time, Nekrogoblikon and I were on tour driving through the Midwest and I had to take a wicked piss, so we pulled over at a gas station. I ran to the bathroom, and it was locked. There was a sign that said, "ASK FOR KEY." So I did, and the gentleman working at the front said, "Sorry, lost the key." So I had the *courage* to take a wiz in a Mountain Dew bottle in the back of the tour bus. That day, I was a true American hero.

Things change. And friends leave. Life doesn't stop for anybody.

—STEPHEN CHBOSKY

Life *literally* stops for everybody at some point…
News flash, Steve! It's called death!

The big lesson in life is never be scared of anyone or anything.

—FRANK SINATRA

I don't know who this Frank guy is, but he's clearly never seen the movie *Hereditary*. Anyone who says that movie doesn't scare them is a dang liar! So, Frank, check that flick out, and get back to me on your life lesson, bud. Uh, might want to stick to your day job, pal, whatever that is, and leave the life lessons to the professionals... like me. I have my own book now. Which you are reading...

RIGHT NOW!

Good is not enough. You've got to be great.

—SIMON COWELL

But isn't great good? This quote doesn't mean anything. It should be, *Good is great, and great isn't enough. You've got to be* **green***!*

The most important thing is to enjoy your life, to be happy, it's all that matters.

—AUDREY HEPBURN

Try telling that to my landlord, Audrey. All that matters to him is that I pay my rent on time. And by *landlord*, I mean Alex, the guitarist of Nekrogoblikon…since I'm crashing on his couch. Speaking of which, Alex, if you're reading this…I am going to be late on rent this month…sorry.

In the end, it's not the years in your life that count.
It's the life in your years.

—ABRAHAM LINCOLN

I'm going to be completely honest with you…I have no idea what this guy is talking about. His advice is the least valuable of all the presidents…which is why he's on the penny!

We all have two lives.
The second one starts when we realize we only have one.

—CONFUCIUS

More like *confusing*, am I right?

To live is the rarest thing in the world. Most people exist, that is all.

—OSCAR WILDE

Wild thought there, buddy, but I'm pretty sure everyone is alive, unless they're dead. Doesn't seem that rare to me…but what do I know? I just have my own book! When you have a book of your own, perhaps we can talk.

Life is not always a matter of holding good cards,
but sometimes, playing a poor hand well.

—JACK LONDON

I once broke my hand at Chili's in Utah. *Two and Half Men* was playing on television, and I laughed so hard I knocked over my margarita. When I stood to clean it up, I slipped on the liquid and broke my hand.

Many people are afraid of the dark,
but the real tragedy is those who are afraid of the light.

—PLATO

The *real* tragedy is that people are claiming not to be afraid of the movie *Hereditary*—and I'm not even getting into the hereditary conflicts that exist between this guy and Neoclassicists who can't mix comedy and tragedy, 'cause that just isn't even funny. But, seriously, what are these people trying to prove? Do they think it makes them tough? I don't know about you, Play-Doh, but I don't trust *anyone* who claims that movie isn't scarey. Possessed little children getting their heads friggin' knocked off?

No, thank you!

In every life, we have some trouble,
but when you worry you make it double.

—BOBBY MCFERRIN

Doubles are great!
Double vodka tonics, double burgers, double dare...you know what they say, two heads are better than none.

CHAPTER TWO

Work

BACK ON MY HOME planet, we would all pitch in to make sure our planet was clean and self-sustaining. If we wanted food or goods, we would just trade or barter, always ensuring every goblin had enough to survive. On *this* planet, that's called a "cult," or being a "dirty hippie," and it all seems very frowned upon. Here, especially in America, you have to a get what's called a "job"—something screamed at me most when I first arrived on this planet, which all seems very odd now since people first screamed at me to *get* a job...and now they're screaming at me because I'm *taking* their jobs.

To be completely honest, I wish someone would *take* my job. It's the *worst*. I sell *insurance*. From what I've gathered sitting at the bar on breaks and after shifts, scrolling social media...*everybody* on this planet hates their job, and every job on this planet is *the worst*. It's so bad, apparently, that employers literally have to pay people *money* to work these jobs.

So over the countless hours I've spent working, I've discovered a few job hacks that will help you become a Job*master*...which will, in turn, make the day go by *faster*! (*Rhyme! That rhymed. This book is writing itself. Maybe next I'll try poetry.*)

Anyway, here is how to work *smarter*, not *harder*. (*Ooh! Did it again and I definitely made up that saying!*)*

*Editor's Note: John Goblikon did not come up with the saying "Work smarter, not harder."

CREATE A SCHEDULE

Just like anything, you need to prioritize to maximize your day. Start with your "in time." When you're "supposed" to be at work.

IN TIME: Morning-*ish*

I like to think of this as a mere suggestion. After all, time *is* merely an illusion, and it's elastic. Don't let *it* run you; *you* run it. (Unless you're, like, an hour late, then you *should* actually run. *Run like hell! You're so close to being fired! RUN!*)

I'll get to some great excuses for being late…a little later in this chapter. I guess you could say that I'll be a *little late* with the *late talk*. (I'm really getting the hang of this being-such-an-amazing-writer thing.)

Anyway, next, map out all the things you need to accomplish in the day. *Number* them. Also, it's very helpful to list them from *best* to *worst*—or *most fun* to *truly not fun at all*.

For example:

TO-DO

1) Chili's happy hour
2) Scroll Instagram on toilet
3) Nap under desk
4) Look up new jokes
5) Tell new jokes to coworkers
6) Watch as those jokes absolutely crush…and your nickname of "The Jokeman" grows into folklore
7) Make a meme
8) Call a friend at their job, so you both can pretend to be "potential clients" for each other…but really you're both working together to figure out that last season finale of *True Detective*
9) Make funny faces in the bathroom mirror
10) Do actual work

Don't beat yourself up if you can't complete all the tasks. So you only got one through nine done...*that's okay!* Be proud of the things you *did* accomplish. Remember, 53 percent of workers say they are unsatisfied with the recognition they get at their job, which basically means 47 percent were lying. That means it's up to *you* to properly shed praise on all your accomplishments.

COMPLIMENT EXAMPLE

"Nobody can sneak-eat an entire burrito
in a bathroom stall like you!"

Don't be the *best*; don't be the *worst*. If you're the *best* at your job, you're just going to get more responsibilities...and that means more stress! If you're the *worst*, you'll probably get fired, and then you'll have to start this whole shitty process over again! Just...

BE MEDIOCRE

This is also good mantra to have with your coworkers, as well. It's okay to talk with them in the break room, or eat lunch with Phil, because it *just barely* beats eating alone. Don't ever make that transition from *coworker* to *friend*. You want to be able to make your work environment pleasant during the week, but on the weekend you'll still want to be the weird, wild stallion you really are and not have anything brought back into the workplace. You know what the most awkward day of work is? The day *after* the holiday party, because now you have to stand by the water cooler and pretend like Caroline from accounting wasn't doing the splits on her desk while simultaneously vomiting and singing Jon Bon Jovi songs to impress the guys in the mailroom. Avoid making *that* a regular occurrence—and also never, *ever* go out with your boss!

Brad: "Hey, John. Want to hang after work?"
John: "Nope!"

Excuses

"Excuses are like assholes.
It's all about the presentation!"

Excuses are these really cool things that, if you get in trouble, or somebody asks you something you don't know the answer to, will immediately help get you out of the jam. People seem to just accept them as
fact. Whether you're late or simply forgot to do something extremely
important, here are a few sure-thing-topics I always like to use:

EXCUSE TOPICS

CAR PROBLEMS. DOG PROBLEMS. BUTT PROBLEMS.
RELATIONSHIP PROBLEMS. FIRE PROBLEMS.

Fire Problems is definitely my favorite. It's a total trump card:

Brad: "Why are you late?"
John: "Fire"
Brad: "Oh, gosh. I hope everything is okay."
John: [*Silence*]
Brad: "By the way, where is that report I asked you to pre-
   pare earlier, John?"
John: "Fire."
Brad: [Thinking] *Well, since it is now most likely burnt to
   ashes, I definitely can't expect one from you.*

See? And if you live in California like I do—oh, man—they don't
even double-take. They know damn well it's possible. Hell, it's more
than likely!

MEETINGS: LEARN TO LOVE THEM

Meetings, much like gas station hot dogs, will sneak up on you unexpectedly. Don't fret, this is actually a blessing in disguise. Can you do work in a meeting? Nope. Your boss will most likely ask—nay, *demand*—your full attention. (Enter *wicked daydream mode.*)

He or she is basically giving you the green light to stare at a spot on their shirt and drift off to your happy place. Sometimes I'll spend all morning thinking about what I'm going to be thinking about during a meeting: a wild-west adventure, an erotic sexcapade, dogs trying to cross the street while wearing tiny shoes! *Your mind is your oyster! Go buck wild!* Just make sure to nod every forty-five seconds, throw in a few *Mmhmm*s and *Oh, okay*s under your breath. And…

DON'T SAY ANYTHING UNTIL THE VERY END

Then, when your blowhard of a boss is done blabbering—*that's* when it'll be your time to shine. You'll quickly turn off your delicious, disorderly daydream (like when your mom just walks into your room without knocking and catches you watching porn), you look around the room at all your yawning coworkers, then back to your sad sap of a boss, and you say: "Well, let's just to take it one step at a time."

It doesn't matter what they were talking about: *Works. Every. Time.*

CHAPTER THREE

Don't Become a "Brad"

WHO IS BRAD? MY boss. *What* is Brad? The worst.

You see, my boss, Brad, gained a very small, like way smaller than me, internet following after his appearance in the Nekrogoblikon music video for the song "No One Survives," a video where he was caught, red-handed, berating me and humiliating me in front of my one true love, adult film star Kayden Kross. (See adjacent photograph taken on the set of the third season of my show, **RIGHT NOW**.) In a fit of rage, I attempted to rip his face to bits… unfortunately, contrary to the song, he did survive…and after many plastic surgeries (Los Angeles is a hell of a place), he returned to, not only, his job as Head of Operations of our insurance company… but also reclaimed his throne as Head of Douchebaggery. His life's mission is to continue to bring me down and make me feel like a total zero.

So, yes, Brad is a real person in my life…but what if I were to tell you that there are Brads in all our lives?

(Yes, the name "Brad" is a common name for white dudes with chiseled features and eyes that lead to nowhere, but I am speaking in metaphors…and I'm pretty sure I'm also speaking in tongues!)

Brads are all over society! Your evil stepdad can be a Brad, the Tinder date who ghosted you also can be Brad…or a Brad can be the barista at your local Starbucks who, every time you order a large coffee, corrects you in a loud, demeaning tone by saying that it's venti. (Oh! Sorry I don't speak German! You are talking to me like this doesn't happens all the time! You are well aware that, in this scenario, a large and a venti are essentially interchangeable—like figuratively and literally. So, since we've already established I need the biggest cup of caffeine juice ya got, why don't you spare me the embarrassment and foreign language lecture! Aka: You're a Brad!)

It's extremely important to be able to identify "Brads," and then learn how to cope with the "Brads" in your life—because unfortunately, they are friggin everywhere!

TRAITS OF A "BRAD"

- Loud talker
- Only laughs at his own jokes
- Brags about how many beers he can drink (e.g. "Wow, a hundred beers? You must have been so fun to be around!")
- Favorite word: "Bro"
- Second favorite word: "Bruh"
- Makes weird acronyms, abbreviations, and rhymes: "Bro, let's GTFO and go skizz on the whizz"
- Insists on only referring to women using animal terms: chicks, cougars, birds, babes, pterodactyls, etc.
- Clothing: Bluetooth, cargo shorts, popped collars, college football hats, shirts with slogans like "I only date models" or "No fatties allowed," sunglasses on back of neck or head; anything Ed Hardy, or any tattoos that looks like something from an Ed Hardy shirt
- Too much "hair product"
- Does CrossFit: You only know this because they tell you every six seconds
- Common phrases: "I'm just playing devil's advocate here" or "You've never been to a Vegas pool party?!?" or "You'd do it if you loved me" or "Hey, John, this is your landlord giving you the fifth and final call, letting you know you will be evicted Friday if you don't pay the last six months' rent…"
- Favorite musician: Doesn't have one
- Laughs like a hyena
- Hurts your hand with a "high five"
- Claims to be a "nerd" because he thinks "that Khaleesi chick from *Game of Thrones* is hot"
- Still uses "dibs" to claim things as his own
- When a work meeting is clearly over, he asks another question that makes the discussion go on for an additional forty or forty-five minutes

You now know how to identify a "Brad" out in the wild, but how will you deal with him? How does one cope with a "Brad altercation?"

Here are a few common scenarios in which you might run into a Brad, paired with a handful of John Goblikon–approved methods to overcome this douchie, douchie, obstacle.

AT A PARTY

Thank Goblin it's Friday! You have a belly full of Chili's, and now you are ready to hit up a party, let loose, and possibly get goblin wasted (in this context, possibly meaning, "Oh, for sure, my dude"). You know everybody's going to be so relieved you've just entered the party zone, so it's time to do a little lap and say hello to all your fans…er, friends. That's when you spot one. Quite possibly, more than one. It could be what we call a "bundle of Brads." They might do one of the following: challenge you to a chugging contest; demand a chest bump; roast you in front of your friends; or even tell you that you have a spot of chipotle mayo on your shirt, then when you look down to where their finger is they'll hit you on your big green nose and start screaming and laughing like they just witnessed a friggin magic trick! Fear not, though. Here are a few surefire moves to get you out of this humiliating situation.

Pretend they are invisible!

Literally. In order for them to hurt you, you first have to acknowledge them. If you see them waving at you, calling you over… look around, look to each side of them, just beyond them, hell, *through* them. Then shrug, as if you may have seen a ghost…or Patrick Swayze…in the distance, or that it must have been a figment of your imagination. If they call your name, suddenly, you can't hear worth a damn! *Must have been all those metal shows! Damn ears.*

This will drive them absolutely bonkers!

Everything a Brad does is geared toward attention. Take that block away from their shitty Jenga tower and watch them crumble!

AT WORK

This one is a tough one, especially if you have a Brad who is your boss...
who's also *literally* named Brad! It's, uh, *the worst*! Luckily, I have a ton
of experience with this. What I suggest here is to become a teenage girl!
Oh, for this one it's not literal...unless that is something you identify as.
I'm not here to judge. That reminds me, this one time I worked with this
guy who identified as a Labrador retriever, weird dude, wouldn't stop
humping my leg and pooping on the conference room floor. When I say
"become a teenage girl," what I mean is, act like you love Brad in front
of him, then once he leaves the room, make fun of him, talk behind his
back, and make sure everybody knows you're just using him. My favorite burn is when I see Brad, I'll go "Uh, hey, Brad, cool shirt." Then he'll
leave the room and I'll turn to my coworkers and say, "*NOT!*" Oh man,
gets them every time. I mean, "Brad tries his best, he really is a good
guy...*NOT!*" See? Did it again.

THE GYM

This place is filled with Brads. Male and female Brads. Grunting, lifting,
checking themselves out in the mirror, asking if you "need a spot." Here
is what I recommend: *Don't go.* Yep. Do not go to the gym. At all. Like,
ever. Not only is it a Brad breeding ground, it's just not a very fun place.
Run? *You* run, pal. I'm not running unless some wild animal is chas-
ing me! Squat? I do those every day in my bathroom, over my toilet.
Burpees? Yeah, I get those after I drink too much beer. All the names of
these places are dumb, too! Gold's Gym? More like *bronze*! Am I right?
LA Fitness..."we have locations all over the country!" Well, uh, then
you better change your name to America Fitness or Earth Fitness...bet-
ter yet, Planet Fitness! Wait, that's the name of a gym already? They've
got smoothies there? All right, I'll give it a shot!

AT SCHOOL

It's pretty obvious why I'm popular with the ladies, but would you believe it I also really have a way with the kids, too! I know how to speak to the youth of today, and let me tell you, Brads form at a young age. They're all over our schools. There should be less focus on this whole D.A.R.E program. Kids gonna smoke what kids gonna smoke. There needs to be more focus on Brads! Change the name to B.A.R.E! Not unlike my favorite Nekrogoblikon song, "Bears."

With these young Brads, you have to strike *first*! If you see them walking your way, full head of steam, you know they're seconds away from stuffing you into that locker. Beat them to the punch. Lather yourself up with a little baby oil and get into that locker! (You'll be safe in there. Plus it's dark. Have yourself a little "you time.") Give *yourself* that wedgie! Steal that lunch money from yourself! Kick *your own* ass! They can't be a Brad to you if you're already a Brad to yourself.

ON A DATE

Ladies, and/or gentlemen, you may be dating a Brad, **RIGHT NOW**! Even worse, you may have married one! First things first, though, dump him, ship him away, sell him, whatever you have to do. There are bigger, better fish…*not* named Brad. I always say, "Why settle for a Brad when you could level up to a John?"

However, if you're not already married to a Brad and you end up on a date with one, this can get a little awkward. He's probably going to do all the talking, bragging about the new (insert dumb car part name) he put on his (insert dumb car name). This is when you do what I refer to as "faking your death." That's right, Shakespeare! Break out those acting chops! It's your time to shine! I find "choking" takes too long. Just a good ole, mid-sentence heart failure should do the trick.

"Brad, what a cool story, golf is absolutely riveting, BUT—" Then you freeze, let your eyes get real big, and fall over to your (fake) death. Brad's are so dumb, they'll have, like, *no* idea what to do. He'll probably cry like a little baby and start Googling "how to revive a dead person." A waiter will then rush over, which is when you'll whisper, "Got a real Brad on my hands here." They'll instantly know what to do. They'll scream for help, accuse Brad of poisoning you, demand he pay the bill and turn himself in to the police…meanwhile, you're getting whisked away by paramedics, who are actually just actors you hired off Craigslist.

As you get to the outside of the restaurant, you hop off the stretcher and make a clean getaway in your brand new sports car. *Shoot!* Forgot to mention that earlier. When you hug Brad hello earlier in the evening, make sure to secretly lift his keys. *You'll need them later to escape in his car you stole!*

CHAPTER FOUR

Reading

WHO THE HELL ACTUALLY *reads*? Are you even *actually* reading this **RIGHT NOW?**

Go listen to the audio version, either as a download from my favorite audiobook company, Recorded Books and Tantor Media— or the limited-edition vinyl audiobook with bonus material from Rare Bird. Just click *this* link.* (Note to Rare Bird: Please add the actual long-ass link to the audiobook here.)

*Note from Rare Bird: We told John that it isn't possible to put a hyperlink in a physical book, but he demanded that we do it...so please just visit rarebirdbooks.com for more information on the vinyl audiobook companion or wherever you typically purchase audiobooks for the full audiobook edition of this book. Click away!?!

CHAPTER FIVE

First Dates

WHETHER IT'S ON TWITTER, Instagram, or when I'm just out among the people of Earth, the most frequently asked questions have to do with dating. I'm constantly amazed that it's already 2019 and the only person people feel comfortable discussing intimacy with is a dang goblin…well, *that* should tell you everything you need to know about the current state of dating. There shouldn't be a need for me to elaborate, but I will.

It's hard, I know. There are apps: Tinder, Grindr, LinkedIn, FarmersOnly, the list goes on. Back in the day, we use to have to walk up to a human boy or girl and use words to communicate as quickly as possible, until eventually we'd vomit on their shoes and awkwardly scream, "Cool, bye!"

However, you've done it, you now have each others' numbers and have begun the *texting process*. A little witty banter back and forth, maybe a pic or two (don't give away too much!), then one of you eventually builds the courage to ask the other on a date. Make it *you*.

Suddenly, they agree to said date. You begin sweating profusely. Your heart beats like a double-bass pedal ripping through (insert Nekrogoblikon song). It's now time for…*the first date*.

Who? What? When? Where? How? So many decisions to be made. Everyone's absolutely terrified of the first date! There's even that horror movie *50 First Dates*, starring Julia Stiles and Keith Ledger. Fifty? No thanks! I don't even want *one*! Well, what if I told you, you never have to go on a first date ever again?

Me? I've never been on a first date. Want to know why? I *always* ask them on a *second* date, first!

I know what you're thinking: *Uh...but, John, how can we go on a second date if we've never been on a first date?*

Oh, ye of little knowledge about date stuff. You having never been on a first date, welp...that's a little secret that only you know and don't have to share with anybody else. Actually, don't tell anybody, ever! That usually bums them out, and then they get all weird and say they can never trust you again and eventually you aren't legally allowed within fifteen feet of their workplace.

I always just start by saying, "Would you like to go on a second date with me?" They'll likely say, "Uh, we've never been on a date before," which is when you'll say, *"Ouch.* You don't remember? I mean, I thought it went pretty well, but I guess that makes one of us." If you *really* want a slam dunk, though, whip out that photo you superimposed of their head on your grandma's body from that one pic of the time she took you to Dave & Busters for your birthday. *This will seal the deal.* They'll be so embarrassed they didn't remember, they may even decide to treat *you* for date number two.

There's also a chance that, when you ask them on date number two, they'll assume they have in fact been on a date number one with you. (It's 2019, dating has become a game of quantity over quality!) Then, *boom!* You're suddenly on your way to date number *two*, with none of the pressures of a *first date!*

I know! MIND. BLOWN.

No need for small talk about your favorite color or if you've ever watched *The Wire.* You're well on your way to a real, genuine conversation about in-depth topics that actually mean something, like who has more followers on Instagram.

After all, the pressures of a first date are all mental and self-inflicted. This is a gift for you as much as it is for them. So, after you have a killer date number two, you know what that means? Yep. You're in a full-blown, serious, committed relationship, and you're ready...for the next chapter! (Figuratively, but also—according to *Merriam-Webster's* 12th Edition—literally. Just turn the page, please.)

CHAPTER SIX

Relationships

I ONCE READ THAT the key to any good relationship is spontaneity. So, that being said…*never* be yourself. Try an accent, or a disguise, but always keep them guessing.

"I'm not your boyfriend. I'm an Italian boat guy. Want to go for a ride in this Hyundai gondola?"

See? Easy.

Speaking of Hyundai…relationships are kind of like cars, if you think about it—*which you should, because you'll see this is a dope transition.* For them to run smoothly, you have to maintain them. Sometimes they need to be fixed, and sometimes they just need you to clean out all those Monster and Red Bull cans in the back seat…or put your CD case…*literally* anywhere else—since your car doesn't even have a CD player, apparently.

*Note, if the Hyundai Elantra people are reading this, that it would be reeeeeal cool of you to allow the radio box to take my CDs again. This Hootie & the Blowfish Greatest Hits disc ain't gonna play itself!

Now back to owning a car, I mean…*relationships.* Like a relationship, owning a car is expensive and can prove quite difficult, but this is what you signed up for at the dealership, so you better be willing to give it what it needs to run or be prepared to get through life on a skateboard. (Skateboards *are* rad, but they're built for one person, which means you'll always be alone—unless you have tiny feet. Most likely, though, it'll be you doing kickflips by your damn self. Alone. Also, it's kind of hard to Netflix & Chill if you're alone. I speak from experience. Watching *My Big Fat Greek Wedding* and *My Big Fat Greek Wedding 2* with a skateboard gets old real fast.)

Also, when I refer to "relationships," that doesn't have to be interpreted as anything romantic. Friends are also in relationships with you: you vent to them about work, they hold you when you stub your toe on the coffee table and cry, and they lie about liking your new haircut because they're still trying to figure out if you're doing it as a joke or if your hairdresser was blindfolded.

That being said, here are the Dos and Don'ts of relationships:

DOs

Check In
This is your responsibility as much as theirs. Drop a little line and say hello once in awhile. Oh, and Phone Calls > Text.

"Like" Their Dumb Posts on Social Media
Somebody has to!

Ask How They Are Doing
If you only want to listen to yourself talk, start a podcast! (Which BTW, I have, and it will be available everywhere soon!)

Pretend to Listen
Listening to anybody for more than five minutes is damn near impossible! People just want to think you are listening, just smile, nod, and say, "Well, you just gotta take it one step at a time."

Compliment Them
Ladies, dudes, kids, adults, plants, goblins...*everybody* loves a compliment! It just makes them feel good inside. The vaguer the better! Like, "I love those shoes" is fine, but something like, "Hey, I just wanted to tell you, you're really doing it and I think that's awesome," will go a lot further...mostly because they will spend the entire rest of the conversation trying to figure out what the hell you were referring to, which should open up a lot of time for you to talk about yourself again.

Physical Attention

First and foremost, this is only if there is consent here, can't believe I have to write that, but we live in a world of trolls…pervy, pervy, trolls. A hug, a kiss, a handshake, or for my germaphobes out there, a fist pound. (I mean, people touch their genitals with their hands, then they wonder why I don't immediately want in on that action.)

No, thank you!

Acts of Service

Do something special for *them*, and *only them*. Not when *they* ask, though. I never do anything once somebody asks me. When you love somebody, you should always be thinking: *What does this person want or need?* Kayden Kross, for example. Yes, pornstar, global icon Kayden Kross…from the Nekrogoblikon video "No One Survives"…starring… me, John Goblikon, viral sensation…took the web by storm. I felt the connection, both in front of and behind the camera, and I know what she needs…*constant DMs of everything I'm doing.* Made a sandwich? *DM.* Drove by a gym. *DM.* Feeling cute. *DM.* I know that when I see "blocked" after I've sent her a DM, she's seen it, she appreciates it, and that she wants more…and she *will* get more.*

Note from Rare Bird: Legally and ethically, we've tried to explain to John that continuing to DM people like Kayden Kross after they've blocked him could be construed as harrassment and we can't condone or support this type of behavior.

DON'Ts

Forget to Respond to a Text

"I didn't see your text!"…says the person who checks their phone every friggin' minute!

Post a Picture or Video of Them Wasted

Maybe this is the insurance salesmen by day, metal goblin by night, speaking…but it's really hard on a Monday trying to explain to Brad why I was claw-deep in margaritas when I was *supposed* to be "working from home." That's on you, Pete, from accounting! Way to be a rat! Goblins > Rats, too.

Ruin Their Birthday Party

Apparently, here on Earth, having a birthday is a *huge* accomplishment, and it's basically like *The Purge*, where if it happens to be your birthday you have a free pass to do and act however you please. So…*let them!* Look, I've dressed up in a theme, dumped bodies in a river, and even gone out to see David Lynch movies for peoples' birthdays…like, is that point of the movie to confuse me and make me regret not seeing *The Fast and the Furious 16*, because it worked, David! If it's *their* birthday, be a team player, really *play ball*, be a good sport, and (*Note to Rare Bird: Please insert some other sport reference!*)

Speak Ill of Their Family

"Speak ill of their family"…uh, who talks like that? I know Rare Bird is helping me sound like an "author," but that's a little over the top, ya? I guess it's chill if people think I'm like Bill Shakespeare. So, with their families…don't hate on them! Even if their family totally sucks, because they share a few chromosomes, they will die defending each other. It's a battle you will *never* win. Creating a fake Facebook account and absolutely *roasting* them in the comment thread is totally fair game though!

Scroll Through Their Photos Too Fast

If somebody hands you their phone to look at a photo, you should look only at that photo they have set up for you to see. I've been on both sides of this, and they can both get pretty awkward. If I'm trying to show you this handsome pic of me crowd surfing at one of Nekrogoblikon's shows in Germany, *don't suddenly start scrolling left, okay?* I was in a vulnerable place in my life and thought lingerie would help hide my hump. On the flip side, I have been handed a phone by an old lady-fan to see a John Goblikon blanket she knitted, only to flip too many times, revealing what can only be described as *a vortex of wrinkles!* Almost lost my appetite for human skin right then and there…*almost.*

Wake Them Up

Nobody likes to be woken up. *Nobody.* Especially your loved ones…and yet, I can't even tell you how many times I've heard: "John, wake up!" or "Get up, John, it's time for the show!" or "Wake up, you're driving!" or "Sir, you can't sleep here this is a public restroom!" It's just no fun.

Let. Them. Sleep.

Are relationships easy? *No.*
But neither is anything that's worth a damn in this life.
Don't be easy, **STAY HARD.**

CHAPTER SEVEN

Writing

"People say, 'What advice do you have for people who want to be writers?' I say, they don't really need advice, they know they want to be writers, and they're gonna do it. Those people who know that they really want to do this and are cut out for it, they know it."

—R. L. Stine

I LOVE R. L. Stine. I love him so much, in fact, that every time I read his books I get *GOOSEBUMPS!*

Weird name, though. RL's parents must have been exhausted at that hospital:

> Nurse: "I need his name for the birth certificate."
> RL's Mom: "Oh, jeez. Caught me off guard...R?."
> Nurse: "The name has to be more than just one letter."
> RL's Dad : "Okay...how about RL?"
> NURSE: "That'll do!"

How did *I* know I was destined to write a book? There was this magical ringing I kept hearing. It got louder and louder. *Was it in my head?* No. *My ears?* Didn't believe so. *My pocket?* Yup. That's where it was coming from. My phone was ringing. So I took it out of my pocket, answered it, and on the other line was fate...or was his name, Nate? *Yeah, Nate!* From Rare Bird, a book publishing company, telling me they wanted to throw a bunch of money my way just for writing some book. So, I was like, "Uh, yeah...sure." That's when I knew I was destined to be a writer...because I had to. They literally had me sign a legally binding contract...and, so, here I am. A *writer*. An *author*. An *icon*.

I'm going to be honest, though, when I was asked to write this book, I was a little surprised...to find out that people still *read* books, but also because I consider myself more of a metal-mascot-icon-internet-famous-goblin-sex-symbol than an author. I knew I had a lot of work to do, I didn't just want to write any ole book. I wanted to write the *best* book, and become the greatest writer since whoever wrote *Everybody Loves Raymond.**

Note to Rare Bird: Everybody Loves Raymond *was a CBS sitcom based around comedian Ray Romano, created by Phil Rosenthal, with a staff of about forty-one different writers.*

I knew right away I had to get to the place where all great ideas come from, the absolute writer's mecca: Starbucks. Apparently, office space is very cheap there since all the best writers in the world go there, grab a latte, head to their designated desk/coffee table, open up their laptops, and begin their next great artistic contributions to society. There I was, Pumpkin Spice Latte in hand, my Dell desktop barely fitting on this stupid, tiny, wobbly table, wondering why the Wi-Fi password needed to contain so many freaking lowercase and uppercase letters—*and don't get me started on the symbols!* ("StAr-BuCk$$$" should have known!)

I was ready to write the next great book…but *how*?

"Seriously, dude. How do I write?" I said to the long-haired, beanie-and-Che-Guevara-shirt-wearing hippie next to me. He took off his four-hundred-dollar Beats by Dre headphones, gently placed his vape pen on the corner of the table, and—speaking in a voice that sounded like he just gargled ocean water—said: "You're a writer? *No way! Me too, bro!* You have to read *The Artist's Way: A Spiritual Path to Higher Creativity* by James Cameron…then take ayahuasca in the desert!"

I knew I had to be back to work soon, so instead of ayahuasca, I took an Advil I found on the floor and I added an "s" to desert, transforming into a dessert, which I ate. I deserved that Cake Pop. Next, I was supposed to read a *whole* book? Not a chance, so I utilized my friend Siri to research for the *Artist's Way* book. That's when I came across this quote from the author, James Cameron (not to be confused with the director of *Avatar*, *Titanic*, and *The Terminator*—different guy, apparently):

"We've all heard that the unexamined life is not worth living, but consider too that the *unlived* life is not worth examining."

Then, this one:

> **"Anger is meant to be acted upon.**
> **It is not meant to be acted out."**

And this one:

> **"The heart of creativity is an experience of the mystical**
> **union; the heart of the mystical union is**
> **an experience of creativity."**

Are you thinking what I'm thinking? Yup. Writing is just saying one vague statement, then saying that statement again but flipping around a few of the words!

> **"The essence of life is not a plethora of spiritual hap-**
> **penings; it's the happenings of spirits that hold**
> **the essence of a plethora of lives!"**
> **—Me**

Nailed it! Writing *is* **easy**. Look…

> **"Uh, 'Chili's is not meant to be enjoyed for,**
> **it's meant to be enjoyed with.'"**
> **—*The Goblin's Way***

Then if somebody asks, "What the heck does that mean?" You blame *them*. "You don't understand it yet…look *deeper.*"

Another Starbucks writer told me to try my hand at *screen*writing, and some book called *Save the Cat*. First off, I'm sorry to say this, but there's no saving him. I ate him. Though after eating the neighbor's cat, I *did* feel inspired to write a few more tweets about how *cool* writing a book is. So maybe that author *is* actually onto something.

That's when I really started digging *deeper* into my writing peers (i.e. competition). Here are the "top motivational quotes from writers" results on Google, as well as a few of my thoughts:

"Read a thousand books,
and your words will flow like a river."
—Lisa See

Uh, sorry, Lisa, but, no thanks. This is 2019, so…more like, "Listen to a thousand *podcasts*, and your *tweets* will flow like Kombucha."

"The first draft is just you telling yourself the story."
—Terry Pratchett

What a loon! Uh, somebody's talking to themselves. *Hey, who am I?* "And that's the story of the *Three Little Pigs*, Terry." I mean, "You tell a great story, Terry!" Other Terry: "No, *you* do, Terry!"

(That's *me* being Terry Pratchett! *Get it?* Hey, Terry, lay off the sauce, pal. See a psychiatrist while you're at it. *This* book has only one author, and *not* the same person.)

"You can always edit a bad page.
You can't edit a blank page."
—Jodi Picoult

That's great advice, Jodi, which is why this next page is…*blank.*

Good luck editing that, Rare Bird!

[This page was intentionally left blank by John.]

"Every secret of a writer's soul,
every experience of his life,
every quality of his mind,
is written large in his works."
—Virginia Woolf

Duh, that's why I am using a **LARGE FONT**!!! Well, *that*, and because my publisher, Rare Bird, contractually obligated me to write a book with a *minimum* of 188 finished pages—which is *also* why I'm including so many quotes and blank pages.

"When your story is ready for rewrite, cut it to the bone. Get rid of every ounce of excess fat. This is going to hurt; revising a story down to the bare essentials is always a little like murdering children, but it must be done."
—Stephen King

I don't know who the hell this Stephen King guy is, but he sounds so freaking metal! "Murdering children"? Whoa, dude. Rock on. Rewrites are tough, like, I'll write something profound and inspiring, then Rare Bird will do some rewrites in order to make it "readable," or "make-sense," then I'll do what Mr. King wanted and I'll just cut all their stuff—leaving, of course, the most crucial parts...*my* stuff.

"Everybody walks past a thousand
story ideas every day.
The good writers are the ones who see five or six of them. Most people don't see any."
—Orson Scott Card

Orson...you're walking by a bunch of "story ideas," huh? Where were you, Barnes & Noble? It's called a bookstore. Well, my book has like twenty-something chapters, each with a hundred great ideas...*oh, I must be the best author of all time!*

> **"There is no greater agony
> than bearing an untold story inside you."**
> **—Maya Angelou**

Apparently, Maya has never tried Red Lobster's breakfast. Huge mistake. *OH. THE. AGONY.*

> **"If the book is true,
> it will find an audience that is meant to read it."**
> **—Wally Lamb**

Now, *here's* a quote I can get behind. If you're reading this, it's because you were *meant* to. Unless you downloaded it illegally! Then you were meant to get yelled at by Lars Ulrich from Metallica. *Napster joke!* (Told you I'd fit one in! Somebody owes me five bucks.)

> **"Write on, write on..."**
> **—Matthew McConaughey**

This one checks out.

So after reading what a bunch of humans have to say about writing, I have come to my own conclusion. Feel free to cut, copy, and paste it as the caption to your Instagram photo of you lookin' cute.

> **"If you want to be a writer, the best time to start is
> RIGHT NOW!"**
> **—John Goblikon**

If there's a story in your heart, it's time to let it out. Who knows? It could be the next *Twilight*, or maybe it's only destined to be a dope-ass tweet. That's okay, too. There is no time, quite like **RIGHT NOW**.

I would apply this not only to writing, but to *life*.

When's the best time to ask out your crush? **RIGHT NOW!**

When should you finally quit that job you're always complaining about? **RIGHT NOW!**

When should you pay that electric bill? Four days after it's due, which is still one day short of when they *could*, technically, turn off your power completely, but not late enough to slap on some bogus late fee.

I'm sure you're reading this book and thinking, *This is like Dostoyévskiy's* War and Peace *meets* The Sequel to the Bible *by Jesus*.

Yeah, actually, it is…but don't let that intimidate you. Let it inspire you. Nobody could have told me a year ago—having only written emails for my boss, Brad—that I'd be an author of a book on the (soon to be) *Rhode Island Times* bestsellers list! Yet, here I am, making my assistant, Jerry, write it…**RIGHT**…**NOW**!

CHAPTER EIGHT

Book Awards

I AM SO HONORED to be accepted and celebrated by the book community with this award!*

Note from Rare Bird: John Goblikon's Guide to Living Your Best Life has yet to win any awards at the time of this printing.

**However, it did end up on a random Swedish blogger's list of "The Three Best Books Put Out by a Goblin in 2019"—it placed third.*

CHAPTER NINE

Hosting (Your Own Show)

WHAT IS A *HOST*?

Well, they can range from being the face of *The Tonight Show* to seating yourself in your favorite booth at Chili's...directly after asking yourself, of course, if you'll be "dining alone, again?"

I've hosted parties, diseases, and now my own internet talk show! It felt like the natural progression. It felt like destiny. From a very early age, I knew I was being called to the screen. I don't want to call it the "big screen" because it really depends what kind of phone you have. Me, I still have a flip phone that doesn't really get the internets. It's just too hard to keep up...iPhone 8, iPhone 9, iPhone X... *What's next? iPhone Y?!?*

More like iPhone...*why?!?* I don't need a new phone. I have this flip phone, and it's *great!*

After the Nekrogoblikon music video for the song "No One Survives" took off, it wasn't really long after that the offers started to come flying in. I'm talking *big time* movie and television roles. I would read the scripts—some good, some bad. There was always a glaring problem, though...*other actors*. Yeah, they'd give me this script and be like, "*You're* the lead John!" And I'd be like, "Then who the hell is *this* guy?" And they'd be like, "That's your *costar*." I couldn't put my finger on it, but something didn't feel right... or *look* right...it might have been his ponytail...or maybe it was something *deeper*.

I went home to process my feelings, which is important to do when making a big decision. I turned on the television to clear my mind. I began channel surfing between the slew of late-night talk shows. There my answer was, staring back at me, with its generic white-guy smile.

Hosting. My. Own. Show.

These guys didn't have *co*stars! They didn't have somebody else's name on the marquee. It was an epiphany like none other, and it was at that *exact* moment I knew I was put here on earth to have my own show.

So I began researching talk shows, which got boring fast. That's when my boneheaded assistant, Jerry, took over and showed me a list of the most-watched shows that all seemed to be named after the designated time they were airing: *The Morning Show, The Afternoon Show, The Tonight Show, The Late Show, The Late Late Show…* That's when I had to ask myself the most important question of my life: "If John Goblikon was to host his own show, what time would people watch it?"

Two words:

RIGHT

NOW

If you've been reading and following along properly, *you, too,* could have your own talk show. But now it's time to give you my top tips on how to be a good host!

Host Tip One: *Treat Your Guests Like Strangers*
Because…they are. Don't get in a car with them. Don't accept candy from them. If they make you uncomfortable, ask them to leave…live on television.

Host Tip Two: *Do NOT Research Them*
   a. You'll be disappointed…unless, of course, it's Tom Cruise. That reminds me. *JERRY!* Why can't we get Tom Cruise on the show? Tom Cruise is goblin-height, we both worship aliens, and he's always talking about "going green!" Call his agent, **RIGHT NOW**!
   b. I've started to take these improv classes, and they say you're not supposed to plan anything out. Everything is supposed to be "off the cuff." Well, if that's the case, I can't know anything about my guests before I interview them, now can I?
   c. Research is *so* boring. That's why Jerry exists. Ask Jerry to do it.

Host Tip Three: *Make Sure Your Set Doesn't Fall Apart*

Still working on this one, to be honest. I blame Jerry. I guarantee you Jimmy Fallon ain't spending half his show worrying about whether or not the Party City decor is going to fall on top of Kayden Kross*— costar, along with *me, John Goblikon*, in Nekrogoblikon's "No One Survives" music video.**

*Kayden Kross appeared on episode 14 of **RIGHT NOW** with John Goblikon, *available on YouTube.*

**Note from Jerry: As of this print run, "No One Survives" is at 6,924,002 views on YouTube.*

CHAPTER TEN

Who is Jerry?

WHO IS *JERRY*? *JERRY*?!? What the hell is this about? Oh...this is something *you* put in, isn't it? Well, I'll tell you this...you want to know who *Jerry* is? *I'll tell ya!* He's my *assistant* who should be more worried about what *I'm* telling *him* to type for this book and *less* about trying to steal a chapter so he can make this *all about him!*

NEXT CHAPTER, JERRY!!!

CHAPTER ELEVEN

How to Become "Internet Famous"

I DEBATED FOR A while whether to include this chapter. What if I lay it all out there for you and then suddenly *you* become internet famous—or, even worse, *everybody* becomes internet famous?!? *Then what?* Would that make me a little less internet famous? Would we all question existence, and what it actually *means* to be internet famous? Is it all *relative*? It truly does beg the question: *If a tree falls in the woods and nobody hears it, is it still internet famous?*

So here is what I propose…I will not only tell you the secret to *becoming* internet famous, but I will also give you my step-by-step guide on how to *become* said internet famous…*under one condition*: that you only use your internet fame for good…*and you will Venmo me 25 percent of all future earnings.* 'Cause I got news for ya…if *you* become internet famous, it's only a matter of time before Rare Bird gives you a call *begging* for a book. *Trust me.* You'll need to be prepared. *So*…here's how to get there…the promised land of the internets…

Step One: *Star in a Metal Music Video That Goes Viral*
(Huge bonus points if it's a Nekrogoblikon video!)
This is really the best way to get your feet wet in internet celebrity-dom. Sure, it'll be a rough three days of acting opposite a smoking hot porn star, but once it's shot and "in the can"—that's a "film" term meaning, once they are done filming, they stick all the footage into one of those canisters and send it up that giant tube, like at a bank drive-thru—the hard work is done. You can sit back, relax, and wait for the views to come in.

Step Two: *Prepare Your Social Media Accounts*
The flood of followers are coming. *Make sure the Twitter levees don't break!* Time to whip out that photo you had your mom take where you thought, *Oh man, that's a cutie right there.* Make it your profile pic. Update your bio to say "internet famous"— maybe have a link to that viral, metal, music video that's gaining views like a car wreck on a highway... and *boom!* You are ready to enter the upper echelon of class, sophistication, and hierarchy that only you and some tween girl in her basement doing makeup tutorials can truly achieve.

Step Three: *Start Touring the World*
If you're not a part of a kick-ass metal band, like I am, then...oh, I dunno, actually. Yeah, see if you can, like, join one? (Just grab a mask and join Slipknot...nobody will actually notice.) So, once you're part of Slipknot, begin touring the world to help build your global reputation. The metal horns are, luckily, universal.

Step Four: *Own Your Own Talk Show, RIGHT NOW!*
Don't star in *my* talk show, *RIGHT NOW! with John Goblikon.* That show already has a host: *me, John Goblikon.* I just mean, don't waste any time starting your *own* talk show. Actually...now that I think about it, if *everybody* starts a talk show, then *my* show will start to seem generic and lose viewers.

NEW Step Four: *Watch* **RIGHT NOW! with John Goblikon** *At Least One Hundred Times*
I just decided *this* is the most important step. *Dammit, Jerry! Why didn't you make this Step One?!?* It's like you're not even paying attention while I'm screaming things at you, while you're writing this book that I'm supposed to write!

Step Five: *Have Really Bad Fan Art Done of You*
I have the greatest fans in the galaxy! Duh. One of the coolest parts of me being internet famous is having people all over the globe send me the coolest fan art they did of me. Yeah, that's right, *me!* I've been a tattoo, a stuffed doll, a painting in a home...and to think my eighth grade teacher told me that, because I had no friends and ate lunch in a cage, I'd never be loved. Well, *technically*, I still only feel comfortable eating lunch in a cage, but at least now it's a *choice!* Also, PLLLLLLLEEEEEEE-ASE keep making and sending cool fan art of me. It warms my goblin heart and makes me dance that much harder on stage!

Step Six: *Write a Book!*
Even if you can't write, or even spell, if you put your mind to it, you can have someone else write the book for you!

Step Seven: *Have That Book Win a Bunch of Awards*
At this *exact* moment, I haven't even finished this book, so the only award it can win is an Oscar or something. I imagine, though, that once the *second* book is released, or maybe as you're reading this **RIGHT NOW**, you're utterly impressed and overwhelmed at all the awards it will clearly win. (Come to think of it, Jerry, we should devote a whole chapter to the awards* this book *will* win!

*Note from Jerry: See earlier chapter on book awards

You may be saying, "John, that's only seven steps. What's next?" Well, my child, the rest of the steps are up to *you*. You could say *those* chapters have yet to be written. It's a choose your own adventure... or the main menu on Netflix. *The choices are infinite.* You now have the internet fame, don't abuse it...but, also, like, don't ever wait in line for a table at a restaurant, or watch a concert amongst the laypeople*—and *for sure* have it be your opening line when trying to pick up somebody way more attractive than you...after all, you *are* internet famous now.
You're welcome.

CHAPTER TWELVE

How to Live on a Budget

You'd think because money is **green** that I'd have an easier time with it—which is, unfortunately, not the case. I have discovered you filthy humans not only desire cold, hard cash, you're utterly infatuated with it. Your world runs on it, er, rather, it runs your *world*. I get it. What can you buy *without* money? Love? *Uh, good luck with that, Romeo!* Happiness? *Google "poor people"—they're always frowning.* Now, Google "British Billionaire Richard Branson"...*ear-to-ear, all smiles, all the time.* Though, you'd think with all that money he'd be able to get laid. Even his airline company is making fun of the poor guy...*Virgin* Airlines. *Ouch.*

"Mo Money Mo Problems" is one of my favorite songs, *but* the one thing that the song gets wrong (*another rhyme!*) is everything about the whole money part: mo money actually equals *less* problems.

If you're like me, you work a full-time job you can't stand, only to barely makes ends meet, earning a paycheck that arrives on Friday only to be spent by Monday! Bills, food, bills, ganja, bills, Chili's, bills, bills, and more bills! It's an endless cycle. *This* chapter will help you learn to budget your spending—but, more importantly, it's going to take you out from under the burden of money to show you how to befriend it.

Get cool with cash.
Be buds with bucks.
Snuggle those stacks.
Learn to love that loot.
Stay on the good side of greenbacks.

By the end of this chapter, you'll be saying, "Ooh la la" to moolah-lah. (*Note to Rare Bird: Please insert Emoji Wearing Sunglasses.*)

LIVE GREEN TO MAKE GREEN

Housing

Crash on someone's couch! They'll love it! Ask any band member of Nekrogoblikon. When I am staying rent-free at your home, I'm like the gift that keeps on giving! I help clean the kitchen by eating your food! I help with the dishes by adding to them which gives you something to do...*the dishes.* You won't even know I'm there, because I'll be soaking in the bathtub 90 percent of the time (the other 10 percent will be spent giving your toilet a run for its money).

Food

I have yet to buy a single thing at Costco, but I've eaten enough free samples there to feed all of Coachella. It *definitely* could've fed all of Fyre Festival. Did you see those documentaries? I mean, how did that happen, seriously? (Ja Rule, if you're reading this, pal, I'm open to different business ventures, actually. Okay, get this, it's an app...to help you *find* an app. You know when someone's like, "Hey! You gotta try this Uber thing!" and I'm all like, "Cool, but where the hell is it?" Well, with *my* app—*our app*—we'll be able to search, find, and use any app, anytime, **RIGHT NOW!** *Text me when you get out of jail, Mr. Rule!*)

Now, the key to getting multiple free samples at places like Costco or Trader Joe's is *acting.* That's right. Otherwise known as *talking with an accent while wearing a disguise.* Let me show you how to get as many free samples as your green heart desires. Try something like, "Hola, Misseur, this Italian cowboy would like to try a mozzarella stick!" Moments later, show up again with a scarf around your head and a southern drawl, saying something like, "Us ladies from New Orleans can't get enough of these fried cheese logs from It-aly!" And *just like that,* a *free sample* becomes a *free meal,* which saves you money—and *money*...is not free! *You're already saving a ton!*

Parking Tickets
Don't pay them. Simple. *Next!*

Presents for Loved Ones
It's the thought that counts...so think of the first thing you can get for free, and give it to 'em! Snag sugar packets from a diner, fill a water bottle with soap from the bathroom at Starbucks, order a Sears catalogue, so on and so forth... But if you're *really* strapped for time, *get them absolutely nothing!* Then, when the occasion arrives (i.e. birthday, Christmas, funeral...shoot them a text that says, *Did you get my present?* They'll reply *no*, then reply back [in almost caps]: *DANG FedEX! MUST'VE GOT LOST IN THE MAIL! Well, keep an eye out for it.* Soon their eyes will get tired and they'll forget about it, but they won't forget texting with you, and it's the *thought* that counts!)

Bills
Refer to *Parking Tickets*.

Clothing
I find that the lost and found at ski resorts have the highest fashion options for both a night out on the town or that business-casual look that says *I'm gonna sell you something you don't need.*

Transportation
Use the Nekrogoblikon Business Credit Card and get an Uber account. *Music...* It's free. *Porn...* It's free. *Happiness...* It's free! *

*Unless you're sad, which you won't be after you complete my guide to living your best life! Which will make you *happy! And happiness is free.* Well, you *did* have to purchase this book to live your best life, and become happy...so, I guess, technically, happiness costs as much as this book costs.

OPINIONS ON BUDGETING AND MONEY
FROM OTHER INTERNET-FAMOUS PEOPLE

**"A wise person should have money in their head,
but not in their heart."**
—Jonathan Swift

That's the dumbest thing I've ever heard. If you have your money inside you, you can't spend it. I find it is best to keep your money in your pockets or in a shoebox under your bed, and by bed I mean the couch you are crashing on in some random city because 85 percent of the year you are on tour with Nekrogoblikon.

"Money often costs too much."
—Ralph Waldo Emerson

Ain't that the truth! Bitcoin is *far too expensive!*

"A nickel ain't worth a dime anymore."
—Yogi Berra

A nickel was never worth a dime, right? Am I crazy? What the heck does this mean? Also, nice name, Yogi…did you think of this nickel and dime concept while at yo*ga! Get it?* 'Cause Yo*gi*…yo*ga*!? Oh, what's that Yogi *bear*?! *Roasted him!*

**"Money never made a man happy yet, nor will it.
The more a man has, the more he wants.
Instead of filling a vacuum, it makes one."**
—Benjamin Franklin

Oh, man. I need to make some money to buy a new vacuum. Last night, I got home from a very productive day. I woke up. Worked out. At the gym. Well, it wasn't a gym in the traditional sense. I ran laps around Chili's while I waited for it to open. It was more of a power walk. Fast paced. While checking Instagram. Anyway, they opened up. I got in a quick post-workout protein shake to go. You know, Southwestern

Egg Rolls to go, blended using the office paper shredder. Chugged that down. Worked. Pooped. Worked some more. Told a really fun joke to Bill in the cubicle next to mine. *He loved it!* Left work. Went home. Then, as I was getting undressed to get in my pajamas, I knocked over my bong. Not my small bong, but the big one. It's a three-footer made of glass. So, I tried to vacuum it up and it broke my darn vacuum.

"Empty pockets never held anyone back. Only empty heads and empty hearts can do that."
—Norman Vincent Peale

Really? Another quote from someone who doesn't understand that money can't be inside you, because if it was *inside* you, you wouldn't be able to spend it!! Who is paying these people to write this garbage?

"It's good to have money and the things that money can buy, but it's good, too, to check up once in a while and make sure that you haven't lost the things that money can't buy."
—George Lorimer

Nekrogoblikon was playing a show in Montreal and I found this sweater in the lost and found at the venue and it was *so* funny. It said: **I'M WITH STUPID**, then it had an arrow pointing to the left. I took so many selfies standing next to the lead singer of Nekrogoblikon, Scorpion. Everyone loved it! Then, a week later I got drunk and lost it. Everyone was bummed. The band told me it was one of a kind and irreplaceable. *I guess some things…money can't buy.*

"If all the economists were laid end to end, they'd never reach a conclusion."
—George Bernard Shaw

Let's just say every time I get laid, *I reach a conclusion!*

> **"Innovation distinguishes between a leader and a follower."**
> **—Steve Jobs**

Follow the Leader is my favorite Korn album, too, Steve!

> **"Investing should be more like watching paint dry or watching grass grow. If you want excitement, take $800 and go to Las Vegas."**
> **—Paul Samuelson**

You know the old saying, *What happens in Vegas, stays in Vegas.* Well, it's true. Last time Nekrogoblikon played Vegas I lost the band's credit card at a "strip club." I thought a strip club was like an all-you-can-eat *chicken strip* buffet, and let me tell you I was *sorely* mistaken. There was no food there, and the service was *horrible!* Everyone working there was just dancing. I'm all like, "Excuse me, Mr. Fireman. How late are you serving dinner?" He just took of his shirt and *threw it in my face!* Two stars on Yelp, for sure!

> **"Every time you borrow money, you're robbing your future self."**
> **—Nathan W. Morris**

Jeez, another stupid quote. Where do we find these guys? Borrowing money is *awesome!* You go from being completely worthless to having worth! It's amazing, quick, easy…and best of all, *it's free!* "Robbing your future self"? Haven't you seen *Back to the Future*? I'm pretty sure everything worked out great for everyone in that doc. Two more movies, a ride at Universal Studios, flying cars…what have you done, Nathan? Maybe you should *borrow* **some money to** *purchase* this book and learn how to *make* some real money.

> **"I have not failed.**
> **I've just found 10,000 ways that won't work."**
> **—Thomas A. Edison**

You and me both, Tommy. I cannot get this damn Apple TV to pair with my flip phone! I've tried everything! Thinking about returning the damn thing and going back to cable. If I miss another episode of *The Bachelor* and have to hear about it at the office, *I'm going to lose it!*

> **"If you don't value your time, neither will others.**
> **Stop giving away your time and talents.**
> **Value what you know, and start charging for it."**
> **—Kim Garst**

Couldn't agree more, Kim. My time and talents are of *great* value, and I'll charge *you* for it. Specifically, forty dollars for a personal shout out on cameo.com!

> **"Don't tell me what you value, show me your budget,**
> **and I'll tell you what you value."**
> **—Joe Biden**

Here's the thing, Joe. The budget for this book…I spent it all. So, I can't show you anything. *But* I'll have a budget soon because money is about to pour in…and I can tell you one thing, it's *not* from this book… It's from my new *side hustle*. Everyone has them now a days. Like Kanye makes shoes, but his side hustle is being on reality television with his wife, Kim. You get it, right? So, I got this buddy Bill at my office and he filled me in on this great opportunity. See, Bill sells herbal soap on the side. Then I *buy* Bill's herbal soap off of him, which he gets a kickback for. Then I have to find someone—like Bill's ex-wife's new husband—to sell the herbal soap to…then ol' John Goblikon gets a kickback. Then he buys *my* herbal soap to sell *his* herbal soap to an herbal soap connoisseur. *This is confusing, huh?* I'm kind of a visual learner, so think of it all like a food pyramid (refer to upcoming Chili's chapter). It's sort of like that. So, Joe, DM me if you want to sell herbal soap and make some money! *Herbal Soap 2020!*

**"If you live for having it all,
what you have is never enough."
—Vicki Robin**

You and me both! I've been saving up to buy a Nintendo Switch for, like, three years now, and every time I get close to having enough money... Chili's happy hour gets the best of me, and I spend too much, setting myself back. It's tough because, you know, it's *always* happy hour at Chili's. What do they expect?

CHAPTER THIRTEEN

Food

REFER TO THE *NEXT* chapter.

CHAPTER FOURTEEN

Chili's
(Food Pyramid)

IN ORDER TO SURVIVE, we must eat. Well, in the end, as we all know from Nekgrogoblikon's video, *no one survives*. But in order to stay alive as long as possible, we must eat food. To understand how to live your best life through food, let me take you back to 1975.

In 1975, the Vietnam War ended.

In 1975, Steven Spielberg's *Jaws* became the first ever blockbuster hit.

In 1975, *Wheel of Fortune* premiered on NBC.

But most importantly, in 1975, a Texan by the name of Larry Lavine opened an American casual eatery featuring mouth-watering Tex-Mex cuisine…and this establishment was called Chili's… and the world was never to be the same.

"I want my baby back, baby back, baby back ribs" is an understatement. I want my Chili's all day, every day. Chili's is less of restaurant and more of a way of life. At Chili's, it's happy hour EVERYDAY. Can you believe that? Think about it. What a positive and beautiful way of showing an appreciation for life. At Chili's, EVERYDAY has happy hour. At Chili's, happy hour isn't confined to simply three to four hours an evening, excluding weekends and holidays…it's 365 days a year. Just do me a favor, and look at your calendar…*seriously*. Put this book down and check what day it is. I'll wait. Okay, so now you know what day it is. Guess what, IT DOESN'T MATTER BE-CAUSE AT CHILI'S TIME FREEZES LIKE A FROZEN MARGAR-ITA AND LIFE JUST HAPPENS BEAUTIFULLY AND BLISSFUL-LY THE WAY THE CREATOR INTENDED IT OR AS WE REFER TO IT HERE ON EARTH AS HAPPY HOUR. Happy hour at Chili's is more than just a mere corporate tactic to attract customers to purchasing seemingly discounted items in hope they get sauced enough and stay past said happy hour and continue to purchase more and more and more… happy hour at Chili's is the very essence of life… living your *best* life.

We all know life is unexpected. Just like a delectable Southwestern Egg Roll. The idea of a Southwestern Egg Roll makes absolutely no sense on paper. How did an egg roll find itself stuffed with southwestern cuisine? Well, stick a hot one in your mouth and I promise you the answer will present itself all over your taste buds. Apply this same theory to all aspects of your life and you'll be salivating with success!

Now that you understand the beauty and meaning of Chili's as an establishment and a way of life, let me break down for you the food pyramid as it pertains to the Chili's menu—aka the only menu that matters and will ever matter, that is if you decide to apply the teachings of my book and only eat at Chili's from here on out because you *will* succeed professionally, personally, physically, and spiritually if you eat at Chili's. Consider your life: *hacked, saved, and verified!*

Suddenly now I understand why the food pyramid is a pyramid. Start at the top, *then eat and drink your way to the bottom!*

[The Chili's Food Pyramid has been temporarily excluded because Rare Bird still needs to illustrate it to John's standards.]

CHAPTER FIFTEEN

John's Workout Plan

DON'T DO IT!

Or *do*…only if you want to. Don't ever feel like you have to. I mean, that Subway guy* lost a ton of weight from literally walking to eat a big sandwich and look how he turned out.

Editor's Note: We here at Rare Bird do not condone the illegal actions of Jared the Subway guy. We can confidently confirm that John doesn't either, aside from the fact that he finds those old promo photos of Jared with the big jeans hilarious. However, John is, we believe, still somewhat unaware of many details surrounding Jared's actions, not to mention how disturbing they are. It's definitely no laughing matter.

Things That Burn Calories…That Don't Suck

- Rocking out—*metal!*
- Sex/masturbation—*if it feels good, it's good for you*
- Walking to your favorite booth at Chili's—*the one way in the back with the cool lighting*
- Practicing ninja moves in the mirror—*self-defense/self-care*
- Tweeting while walking—*follow me @johngoblikon*
- Avoiding your boss at lunch—*this is like a game of tag!*
- Watching *Two and a Half Men*—*laughing burns calories*
- Getting in an argument with your neighbor—*exhausting!*
- Sleeping—*Break your record! Mine is fifty-six straight hours!*

The *one* thing I can say about working out, is that it's good to get your heart pumping once in a while. Here's a quick way to get that heart *a-thumping*: Go to your local grocery store on Thanksgiving morning. All you need to do is get one friggin' can of creamed corn to make the casserole you found scrolling around on Pinterest (the one you know you're to going to botch), but when you turn down the aisle at the grocery store, it's utter chaos. It looks like a scene out of *The Walking Dead*, but with a dang sale on brains! You get elbowed, nudged, a cart runs over your foot, people are wall to wall, etc., etc. If that doesn't get your heart rate up and give you a killer sweat…then maybe try binge watching *Making a Murderer* (Season One, *not* Two). I mean, *how is that guy guilty!?!?*

CHAPTER SIXTEEN

Smartphone Addiction

MAYBE YOU'RE READING THIS in line at a mom-and-pop coffee shop like Starbucks, or this new hip spot I found on Ventura Boulevard called Coffee Bean, or sitting on the train commuting to hell, or driving to pick up your step-kids. My guess is, in any of those situations, you're most likely reading this on your phone. I mean, I'm pretty sure books don't actually still exist, anyway, and I've been very skeptical of this whole "write a book thing" that Rare Bird is, apparently, according to Jerry, paying me a lot of money to, uh…"write." (Uh, Rare Bird, why don't you just ask me to fax you my book about *fanny packs* and *Beanie Babies*? Can I do that? Should I use my "mojo" that only takes eighteen minutes a page?)

"US adults will spend an average of 3 hours, 35 minutes per day on mobile devices in 2018, an annual increase of more than 11 minutes. By 2019, mobile will surpass TV as the medium attracting the most minutes in the US."

—eMarketer

That means the average person is diddling on their phone for almost four hours each day. *Four hours.* So, I ask you this? Do you want to be average? No? Well, then you're going to have to amp it up, dude! (I use *dude*, but that can mean a *dude* or a *lady*.)

I suggest six hours on your phone a day, minimum. Think of all the fun ways to escape reality! Want to see what your racist uncle thinks of the latest protest? *Facebook!* Enjoy doctored photographs of vain models with inspirational quotes to pair with em? *Instagram!*

Have you ever woken up and said, "I feel *too* good about my-self?" Just sign on to good ole Twitter and let some stranger without a profile pic take you down a peg (or two)!

I haven't even touched on all the cool apps and games yet. As the commercials say, *Want to feel like a crappy cook?* There's an app for that! *Tumblr.*

Want a bunch of teenagers in their basements to be funnier than you? *Tik Tok.*

Want an app that's all about how to find more apps? (Please refer to previous chapter that mentions my future business relationship with Ja Rule.)

You can open them all up and jump from one to another. The possibilities are truly endless! Me, personally, I like to get a real fun-ny snap going on Snapchat. Like, I just ordered food at restaurant, and now, obviously, I have to show everybody that's what I am doing or else they'll just assume I'm dead or happy! Then I'll stroll on over to Instagram to take that same pic, but put a cool new *spin* on it... throw a little sepia here, a little Insta Hefe there, insert quote from Marilyn Monroe...and *booyah!* Things are really starting to heat up! But don't forget to slide in a few DMs before you saunter back to Facebook and share your thoughts on a movie you haven't seen yet...just make sure and remember that art is *not* subjective, your opinion of something is indeed factually supportable (even *without* actual support), and that people who don't agree with your opinion are dumb. They're just friggin' stupid. (Don't forget to point this fact out, of course, in the comments!)

If you haven't reached your full six hours by then, you can al-ways scroll, scroll, scroll. What do other people like and share? What kitty looks best in what tiny sweater? What did Aunt Debra do today at yoga and why can't she let go of the past and realize that, Uncle Ken...? He ain't coming back, which is when I'll usually think of something real funny and go back to Twitter. Get that tweet good and ready... *Don't forget to add hashtags! #Duh #IAlwaysHashtag-John #PrettySureIKnowHowToHashTagAlready #Chilis*

Then you'll inevitably scroll through your timeline and see that somebody's already tweeted that *exact same thing.* Don't panic. Imitation is, supposedly, the highest form of flattery. Simply "retweet" them with the comment, *Uh, totes already tweeted this before. Why don't you try and get a few original tweet ideas, Keith Buckley, lead singer of Every Time I Die (uh, more like...Every Time I RIP OFF JOHN'S TWEETS!)*

Note from Rare Bird: Keith Buckley is the lead singer of Every Time I Die, along with being a published author of ours with his novels Scale *and* Watch. *He and John first met on the set of John's internet talk show* **RIGHT NOW,** *which you can watch online...RIGHT NOW.*

Well, that should do the trick...

See? Staring at your phone is not only normal, it's abnormal! Feel free to do it anytime, anyplace...unless you're with somebody else. Like, anybody.

Wait, you don't look at your phone while another person is present, do you?!? That's literally the worst! Put that dang thing away and try to connect with another *human!* That's what life* is all about! If you're staring at your phone instead of sharing a precious moment with another beautiful creature, life is going to pass you by!

*Please refer to Life chapter

CHAPTER SEVENTEEN

Text Etiquette

I HAVE COME TO the conclusion that, unlike goblins, human beings are not big fans of talking with their mouths. Not much is said face to face. There seems to be an obvious fear of communicating with actual spoken words. Humans almost always much prefer texting. I get it. Why fight that social anxiety of putting on pants, leaving the apartment, and being thrust into a crowd of patrons at some restaurant that Yelp said was, eh, "three stars." You'll only sit across from another filthy human, trying to fight a limited vocabulary to find words, "Hello friend, I've really been dealing with a lot lately and every little thing seems to overwhelm me. Do you want to skip this whole eating-out-in-public thing and go watch some *Home Improvement* reruns on my couch?"

Why?!?

Why put your soul on display like that when you could just send a little ole text that says: *Netflix and Chill?* Your buddy will know exactly what you mean. Then they can just reply: *Yup.* Or if the human language seems too overwhelming, they can simply send a thumbs-up emoji! What a time to be alive—*and filled with public anxieties!!!*

That being said, I have noticed texting can also lead to a tremendous amount of miscommunication. You can't *hear* tone, obviously—unless you ask Siri to read it for you…and let me tell you that lady is *Dead. Behind. The. Eyes.* With all their money, you'd think Apple would have gotten J-Law or Meryl Streep to play Siri. Siri's such a bad actor. What was her direction, "Act like a robot?" If so… *nailed it!*

Luckily for you, I've mapped out the most common texts you will receive, with proper responses to each, assuring you'll never misinterpret a text again. These are fail safe. Trust me.

Them: "You Up?"
You: Always.

Them: "Happy Birthday"
You: "Same phone, who dis?"

Them: "Wanna talk?"
You: "Wanna not?"

Them: "Your Uber has arrived"
You: "Could an adult body fit in your trunk...and can you keep a secret?"

Them: "Call me"
You: "Text me"

Them: "You free tomorrow?"
You: "Let's find out then!"

Them: "Hey"
You: "Whoa, you're a freaking psychopath, please don't ever contact me again with that vague-waste-of-time-intro text I have to sort through in order figure out some meaning."

Them: "What are you doing?"
You: "Texting"

Them: "How are you?"
You: "Follow me on Instagram!"

Them: "Wanna see Nekrogoblikon tonight?"
You: "Duh (rock horns emoji)"

Them: "What's your address again?"
You: "666 Same As It Was When I texted It To You Last Time...Avenue"

Them: "Tell me about yourself"
You: "Google me"

Them: "Gonna be late"
You: "Gonna be eating without you!"

Them: "Did u call me?"
You: "Call me back and let's find out"

Them: "Will u pick a place to meet?"
You: "Rhymes with Billy's"
You: "Chili's"

CHAPTER EIGHTEEN

Scorpion

HELLO THERE!! IT'S ME, Scorpion, and I'm insane.

When John asked me to contribute a chapter to his book, I was gutted. Devastated. At that time, the last thing on earth I wanted to do was write a chapter in a pseudo-self-help manual for the most tragically uninformed and commercially susceptible sub-populous out there: Nekrogoblikon fans (specifically John Goblikon fans). Shortly thereafter, though, I realized that I could use writing this "chapter" as an excuse to drink. So here I am, two beers deep and moving forward with what may be the worst idea I've ever been a part of. But what else is new?

I'm here today to talk to you about negativity, and what I'll refer to as "the need for hate." It's not easy being negative in this posinormative world, but it is entirely necessary. What I'm really getting at here is the tendency for people in our society to blindly push positivity into any given circumstance, regardless of whether or not that circumstance actually *calls* for positivity. There's a time and a place for everything. "Oh, man, I just lost my job, my girlfriend or boyfriend left me, and s/he took the dog and/or kids, but I'm staying positive." Like, fuck you. That's not a situation where one has anything to gain from feeling positive. On top of that, I don't want to hear about it. Negativity serves a valuable function, and that's to create change. If everyone was always positive, there would be no reason for change, because everything would be hunky-dory all the goddamn time. Without change, we'd all still think the Earth is flat, we'd still burn witches, and tritones would be avoided as they're the devil's interval. Plus, slavery. What I'm saying is that by being forcefully positive, you're basically a slaver.

The worst part is that these Posis are coercive. We *trust* them. They put out manuals, blogs, and podcasts to "help those less fortunate" (aka those of us who still don't buy it). In reality, they're simply looking for a quick ego boost—in the form of views, comments, endorsements, free products, etc. To them, humanity has a dollar value. It's arguable that these people actually contribute more to negativity overall than those of us who will just admit when something's not rad. By buying into their garbage, we begin to feel as if our own feelings are invalid, which makes us feel like sad failures, like we can't possibly measure up to these impossible beings. But, no—*they're gonna help you capitalize!* To be your best you! People in the capitalist system are afraid of failure. This is justified because failure can result in a lack of what we call money (an honor system), which basically means you're a slave. The problem is, failure *also* results in innovation, and, you guessed it: change. Failure is not something to be feared. It's part of a system of checks and balances devised by nature itself. I'm perhaps going out on a limb here, but where would evolution be without failure? This is why there's a need for hate. In natural systems, nothing is superfluous. Things may be superfluous for a time, but those things are quickly corrected by Darwinism, at least when you don't try to lie your way out like the Posis. Simply; if hate was ever wrong, why does it still exist? Why does humanity exist? Are we unnatural? Environmentalists will argue that we need to save "nature," but the reality is, we're *part* of nature. The Earth was around long before we were, and it will be around long after we're gone. The Earth does not care if humans die, if trees die, if anything dies. "Save the Earth" is shorthand for save humanity, but thus far all signs point to humanity not being worth saving. If people continue to ignore the hints accessible within a negative perspective, then we will simply perish. A rewarding system is a system which includes failure.

We simply *will* perish, I'm inclined to think. But that's not a reason to worry. Most of us find out about death pretty early on. We're socially programmed to avoid thinking about it, to think about what we *can* do instead of what we can*not* do (i.e. I *can* make money, not I cannot avoid death.) I guess the weird part is that rich people always think they can buy immortality. It's not enough to simply exist—when, in reality, that's our only obvious purpose… *One must achieve it!* I guess that's because it helps people move forward. Our tenacious propensity for positivity is simply another superfluous feature of nature that has yet to correct itself. But alas, maybe things were not always this way. Maybe we've already done this as a civilization… countless times! Aliens! The end.

This has been Scorpion with just enough food to stave off the hunger, and until next time. For thought. FOOD FOR THOUGHT. Peasant.

*Note from John: Uh, somebody needs a little positivity. Scorpion, you should buy a copy of this book. Venmo me!

CHAPTER NINETEEN

Family

FAMILY CAN BE THE relationship that proves toughest to navigate in life. There are designated roles (i.e. mother, father, brother, sister, etc.), but more specifically, there are archetypes, and each member of the family can, from time to time, take on multiple archetypal roles, sometimes all of them. It's kind of like being in a band. The band Nekrogoblikon to be exact.

There's Alex (aka "Goldberg" aka the "Lead Guitarist"), who, most of the time, is happy playing the role of "Dad." He's a leader and a shredder of guitars, who's always putting the band first. He tells us where to be and when to be there. However, he often forgets to take care of himself. The only thing he asks is that, when he gets off work, there's dinner on the table with his favorite beer waiting for him...*ice cold*.

(Thankfully, Chili's is on DoorDash now.) Alex will also lend you money, if you ask after he's had six of those post-work beers. Do something wrong, or talk back to him, and—oh, boy—that's when Dad, I mean Alex, really let's out everything he's kept bottling up all day. Remember to duck and cover. Things *will* be broken.

Then there's the mother figure (aka "Mom"), a sweetheart that everybody loves! She figuratively and literally holds this dysfunctional band together. Keeps it in time. The backbone. Not to mention those long, beautiful, flowing locks. Obviously, I'm talking about the "drummer." I think she loves Dad, but then Dad will mess up a riff on his guitar and Mom will yell something like, "You're not on my tempo, idiot!" Oh, and this one time, I thought it'd be funny to hide that goofy wrench she uses to tighten up the drums. I couldn't resist, I had the best hiding spot...my stomach! That's when our drummer, er, "Mom," came out from the green room, like, "Has anybody seen my drum key?" And I was like, "Uh, did you check the drum-key ring?" *Man, I roasted Mom so hard!* Now, you may be from a family that has *two* dads, or *two* moms—or *no* moms, or *no* dads. *That's totally cool, too!* What's even *cooler*, though, is having siblings. BIG. FAN. *I have four!* Siblings are definitely a huge part of my family.

There's the oldest, the first born (aka the "Rhythm Guitarist"). That role *definitely* tends to get the handsome gene. They'll teach you a few life lessons, a little guitar, and protect you from all the adoring fans dying to meet an internet-famous goblin. He's pretty even-keeled, but behind those baby blues, you know they're still livid they weren't an only child. Expect a solo album from the one most resembling this role. The solo album will come. They can't help it.

Then there's the middle child (aka "The Keyboardist"), the musical savant of the family. *They can play anything!* From chopsticks to (insert a famous keyboard song…I literally can't think of any). Technically, he could be considered the "Funny One," because he'll have you smiling with the way he *tickles* those ivories! He spent hours and hours locked up in his room (he shared with two other brothers) practicing and practicing, because, let's face it, he had to do *something* to stand out or else our parents would totally forget about him. The Keyboardist usually develops some kind of syndrome, mostly due to the neglect, which can lead to demands performing harmonies on songs that don't need them…or, even worse, a keytar.

Then there's the "Mistake Child" who wasn't planned. A few bottles of wine and a Norah Jones album later, then *boom!* Mom is pregnant again, and *this* one is definitely the oft forgotten child because, well, he plays bass. He chose that road himself, of course, so we can't feel *too* bad for him. Bass players (aka "Mistake Children") tend to be like a copy of a copy, in the Xerox sense—never as sharp as the original. I'm sure everybody reading this knows the story of how the idea of the "bass guitar" came to be. Some "Mistake Child" was handed a guitar:

They were given some instructions, like, "Here, learn this instrument."

144

They said, "Six strings, huh? Uh, can I, like, get a version with *less* strings to learn?"

"How about four, dummy?"

Then they agreed, and the "bass guitar" was born, the last member to join the band. I will say *this* about Nekrogoblikon's bass player, though: he *kind of* has goblin hair, which I can really respect. He also seems to deal with allergens well. Yeah, he's allergic to *sleeves!* The guy also wears a lot of cut-off shirts. We can joke like that, we're brothers!

Then, of course, there is the youngest child (aka "Golden Child" aka "The Favorite" aka the "Leader" aka "Nicky" aka "Scorpion" aka "The Singer of Nekrogoblikon"). He's, of course, the brooding, artsy-type, who always yells at you for going in his room and touching his stuff! It's like, I get that you're the singer of the band, bro, but I sleep on *top* of the damn tour bus. Maybe you cut me a little slack. I'm just looking for a blanket. Then he'll usually blow a big cloud of vape smoke in my face and tell me I "just don't get it."

I'll inevitably ask, "Get what?"

Then he'll answer, "Your butt," and laugh and laugh and laugh.

Or he'll run up to you and tell you to pull his finger. (DO. NOT. PULL. HIS. FINGER.) Pretty sure that's what started global warming! It seems he gets it all. The attention. The praise. The front seat in the van. He has style, charisma, and a hell of a metal growl. You want to dislike him, but you can't help but admire him. Even though he's hundreds of years younger than you, you still look up to him. *Literally!* He's way taller than you! Remember not to spend your whole life comparing yourself to this "golden child with a golden voice"...you will always come up short. (*Another height joke?* I can't be stopped.)

Oh, wait. There is one more member of the family I forgot to mention. Me.

The "Adopted Child" (aka the "Stepchild" aka "The Half Sibling" aka "The Band's Mascot" aka "World Renowned Author"). I joined this family late, so I inevitably have my work cut out for me. The family dynamics are already in place.

Where do you fit it?
Answer: The trunk.

Or if the trunk is full with all of those STUPID DRUMS, you will fit nicely on the roof of the car, van or tour bus. It's a price worth paying to arrive in a new city each day with the sole job of rocking people to their core and dancing your green ass off to your favorite band, Nekrogoblikon. This role of the stepchild is actually the most crucial. It's because we have that chip on our shoulder. We go above and beyond to impress stepmom and stepdad! Here on earth, some of the most successful people were stepchildren: Steve Jobs, Marilyn Monroe, Dave Thomas (owner of Wendy's, and the genius who invented the Frosty), Bill Clinton, John Lennon, the Clown from Slipknot, not to mention the most famous adoptee of all time…Jesus.

See? Each family is a hodgepodge of archetypes that you must learn to mesh with. Learn to identify these "family dynamics" early. No matter which category you identify with, don't be afraid to come to grips with the fact you are the black sheep. The outcast. If you're always the one messing things up, chances are, they will not ask you to be in charge of the family BBQ, or play Santa during Christmas, or speak at your Grandmother's funeral. In fact, you can probably skip the funeral all together. Your family won't notice, certainly your Grandma won't! Sure, you may not be showered with love from your parents/band leader like the rest of your family/band, but the lack of responsibility to participate in odd family activities will certainly pay off in the long run!

Finally, the *most* important thing to remember about family: if things aren't working out, you can always get a new one!

There's this documentary about Will Smith's life where he didn't like his family in West Philadelphia, then he moved in with a cooler, much richer family in Bel-Air. It seemed to really work out for him, and he even got his own television show! Then, he lived an amazing life, saving the world from zombies, giants, and even aliens. Some might say it was because he used steroids or B vitamins, but I know…it was because he changed out his family.

CHAPTER TWENTY

Death

NOBODY KNOWS WHAT HAPPENS when we die...except for *Bar Rescue*'s Jon Taffer. I feel like that guys knows something the rest of us don't. Anyway, there's no point in obsessing over death because it's inevitable...sort of like having to take a dump on an airplane. No one *wants* to do it. It's unpredictable and scary. We do everything to try and prevent it, but all we can do is eat a lite meal the night before, wake up early, drink a ton of coffee, empty our bowels the morning of... Sometimes, though, out of nowhere, you feel that rumble in your tummy, like, a thousand miles up in the sky, and you just have to face it. Head on, butt first, you poop on an airplane. Death is *just* like that. Once you embrace pooping on a plane, and that it is a possibility...that it's in the cards...well, then pooping on planes and flying in general gets a whole lot easier. Same thing with death. Accept it, and move on. But, don't *actually* die. Keep reading this book and be a healthy, happy goblin, and live as long as you can. Because we don't know what happens will be like when we die, which is pretty scary when you think about it. Oh, no. I just thought about—*oh my god!*—like...eternal darkness... I need to call my mom. *Wait, my mom is dead!* Now I'm am *definitely* thinking about death. Well, nothing I can do about it, right? My Wi-Fi is cutting out since I'm writing this on a plane and I got to take a dump. BRB.

Editorial Note from Rare Bird: Bar Rescue is an American reality television series about renovating failing bars...and John watches it each night before bed.

Now let's talk about what to do *after* you, or someone you know, dies. It's called Grief, and there are seven stages of it.

They are as follows: *Shock, Denial, Bargaining, Guilt, Anger, Depression,* and *Acceptance.*

Stage One
Shock: I have to poop!? But I did all the proper things to prevent this! How?! Why?! *I'm shocked!*

Stage Two
Denial: Maybe I don't have to poop. Maybe it's just gas. Yeah, it's just the farts, just your run of the mill toots. Nothing *I* can't handle. I am the master of crop dusting. I'll just walk to the back of the plane, dust the entire way, then when I get back there order another Bloody Mary and call it a day. *Goodbye, farts! Hello, smooth flight!* Wait…uh oh, that last fart was undeniably wet…

Stage Three
Bargaining: To all that is Green and Good and Goblin, please do *not make me poop on the plane!* Look, I know I should've probably avoiding ordering that fourth order of Southwestern Egg Rolls over lunch yesterday at Chili's, *but I was hungry!* Okay, if I don't have to poop on this plane, I'll only go to Chili's on days when it's happy hour. That's a fair bargain! (Winky face emoji.)

Stage Four
Guilt: This is your own dang fault, John! And ya know what, it wasn't the fourth order of Southwestern Egg Rolls at lunch, it was the "lite" meal you ate before bed…six orders of Chili's Baby Back Ribs! Come on, man. You already had a giant lunch at Chili's and you *knew* you had this flight! Don't you *dare* try and put this on Chili's, you *know* this is *not* their fault. There ribs are *the* best ribs in the universe, but you must eat them in moderation, especially the night before a flight. Plus, it didn't help that you cut your morning poop short this morning because you spent forty-five minutes in bed watching YouTube reaction clips of kids watching Slipknot music videos. Yes, they are hysterical… but *come on, man!* You knew about this flight for a month!

Stage Five

Anger: *No!* You know what! This isn't my fault. There's nothing I could've done to predict this poop. What the frick!? Why does this *always* happen to me?! I am cursed. That's it! I'm so *angry!!* Ya know, it's just one of those days when you don't wanna wake up. Everything is f*cked, and everybody sucks. You don't really know why but you want to justify holding in your poop for an entire six-hour flight.

Stage Six

Depression: Everything hurts. My stomach feels like it's going to burst, and my butthole is on fire. Each fart is hotter than the last. You know the film *Dante's Peak*? Well, my butt is about to make the Michael Bay remake, like, a thousand miles up in the air in this airplane bathroom. *This sucks!* What's the point of trying to prevent pooping on the plane if it's just going to happen!? It's not fair. This is so depressing.

Stage Seven

Acceptance: I'm going to poop on the plane. It's no big deal. Everybody poops. Hey, poop. I accept you. Thank *you* for accepting *me*.

Then once you've experienced all Seven Stages of Grief, you're ready to embark on the next step in dealing with *Loss*...which is, once again, reading what famous people have to say about it (which is totally legal, because it's in the public domain).

> **"The life of the dead
> is placed in the memory of the living."**
> **—Marcus Tullius Cicero**

News flash, Marcus, when you're dead you're then longer living…so there is no life of the dead. Where do we find these quotes? From the book of the BRAINdead?!

> **"Absolute silence leads to sadness.
> It is the image of death."**
> **—Jean-Jacques Rousseau**

Silent But Deadly is actually my nickname. Not sure what this has to do about dying, other that then when I let a silent one rip on the tour bus, it kills every time! No seriously, we brought our pet hamster on the last tour and one of my farts killed it. RIP Nibbles.

> **"Cowards die many times before their deaths;
> the valiant never taste of death but once."**
> **—William Shakespeare**

You can't die multiple times, contrary to what this Shakespeare guy has to say. Also, Bill, you can't "taste" death. That's unless you're eating at Applebees! (*Chili's for life*—and death!)

> **"While I thought that I was learning how to live,
> I have been learning how to die."**
> **—Leonardo da Vinci**

I'm pretty sure this is a Guns N' Roses lyric… I thought Axl wrote the lyrics, though, not Leo the keyboard player. Wait, is the keyboard player Leo or Dizzy? Who is Leo? Oh, you know what, I'm thinking of the Ninja Turtle, Leonardo. Is *he* still with us or did he die?

> **"Death is not the greatest loss in life.**
> **The greatest loss is what dies inside us while we live."**
> **—Norman Cousins**

If you eat gas station sushi, it will feel like something is dying inside of you.

> **"Guilt is perhaps the most painful companion to death."**
> **—Elisabeth Kubler-Ross**

Elizabeth, I've never died before, but I'm going to go out on a limb here and say that being killed is probably the most painful companion to death, not guilt. I feel guilt every day, and I get over it. Like, do I feel guilty for eating that extra order of Southwestern Egg Rolls? No. I feel guilty for not eating *two more extra orders*, but life moves on. We are all gonna die one day, you gotta. YOLO.

FINAL
CHAPTER

How to Love Yourself

WOW! YOU'VE MADE IT to the end of my soon-to-be-Golden-Globe-Award-winning self-help book, *John Goblikon's Guide to Living Your Best Life*. There's just one final bit of advice I must give, and this advice absolutely *must* be followed, as it's the most important:

GO. F*CK. YOURSELF.

That's right.

No, seriously, pleasure yourself. Whip out your goodies and go for a ride! Think of it more as a reward for finishing this incredible book I wrote for you.

Oh, and take your time! This book isn't going anywhere.

Before reading the final climax of the book, you should reach your own climax.

*Note from Rare Bird: Although we would like you to take John's advice, please do so within reason and respect of the law and others around. If you're reading this book in the comfort of your own home, go nuts.

Okay, now that you've reached your exotic euphoria and cleared your mind, let's wrap this up.

If you take away one thing from this book, it should be that you deserve to live your best life like a goblin. Solely by purchasing this book and spending your hard-earned cash on a guide to life written by an insurance sales goblin/viral star/rock god/author and so on and so forth, that alone speaks in volumes to your open mindedness, compassion, love for life, and lack of inner troll or...Brad. You are GOBLIN. Your skin might be black, white, yellow, or purple*...but under that layer of thick skin, is **green**.

*Note from Rare Bird: If your skin is purple, please call 911 immediately.

Life is what you make it, but you have to earn it. You deserve it, but nobody owes you anything. You have to make it happen for yourself. And you can. You will. Because you are Goblin.

We as Goblins must fight to survive, though, in the end, of course, no one survives...and that's okay. It's about what you do while you are here on this dying planet we call Earth.

So, put this book down. Well, once you finish reading it, get up, and live full goblin. If you fail, or if today just isn't your day...that's all right. There's always tomorrow. Unless there isn't, because you or the planet dies. But hey! You gave it your all. And that's what matters.

Go Green!
Chili's now and forever!
Nekrogoblikon! NEKROGOBLIKON!
Goblins > Trolls.
Your goblin friend till the end,
John Goblikon
@TheRealJohnGoblikon on Instagram
@JohnGoblikon on Twitter
@JohnGoblikon on Tik Tok
@JohnGoblikon on Cameo